Who is your Rabb?

من ربك؟

My Rabb is Allah, the All-knowing

ربي الله العليم

Prolance

www.prolancewriting.com
California, USA
©2017 Bint Abdul Hamid
Illustrations ©2017 Zahra Gulraiz

ISBN: 978-0-9983287-7-5

بسم الله الرحمن الرحيم

This book is an introduction to
Allah's name Al-Aleem, the All-Knowing,
for children.

References to the Qur'an are found at
the foot of each page in order to explore
further with your child and for your
child to develop a close companionship
with the Qur'an.

We advise you as parents to expose
your children to more examples of
Allah's names and attributes, asking them
to ponder on all of Allah's creations.
They are never too young to ponder!!!
Teach the child to live by His names and
remind them that Allah's knowledge
encompasses all things.

May Allah accept our intentions and
yours for His cause. We declare any
errors to be firstly our own and
secondly unintentional. We seek
forgiveness from Allah for our
shortcomings.

Allah
Al-Aleem...

He knows
everything!!

الله العليم ...
هو يعلم كل شىء

How many
creatures
live under
the ground?

كم من مخلوق يعيش تحت الأرض؟

Allah Al-Aleem

الله العليم

He knows

هو يعلم

SURAH AL-AN'AM 6:59

How many leaves fall in the breeze?

كم ورقة يحملها النسيم ؟

Allah Al-Aleem

الله العليم

He knows

هو يعلم

SURAH AL-AN'AM 6:59

When will it rain and where will it fall?

متى ينزل المطر و أين يمطر؟

We can guess

مكننا تقدير ذلك

but only
Allah
Al-Aleem

لا أحد يعلم ذلك الا الله

He knows

هو يعلم

SURAH AR-ROOM 30:48 SURAH LUQMAN 31:34

When will the seed sprout?
When will the fruit appear?
When can I eat it?

متى سينبت الزرع؟
متى ستخرج الثمار؟
متى سأكلها؟

Wait a little while

مهلا

because only Allah
is Al-Aleem

لا أحد يعلم ذلك الا الله العليم

He knows

هو يعلم

SURAH FUSSILAT 41:47

What are you
thinking?

بماذا تفكر؟

What do you
feel?

بماذا تشعر؟

You're not alone

أنت لست وحدك

Allah Al-Aleem

الله العليم

He knows
هو يعلم

SURAH QAF 50:16 SURAH MULK 67:13-14

How many secrets are hidden away?

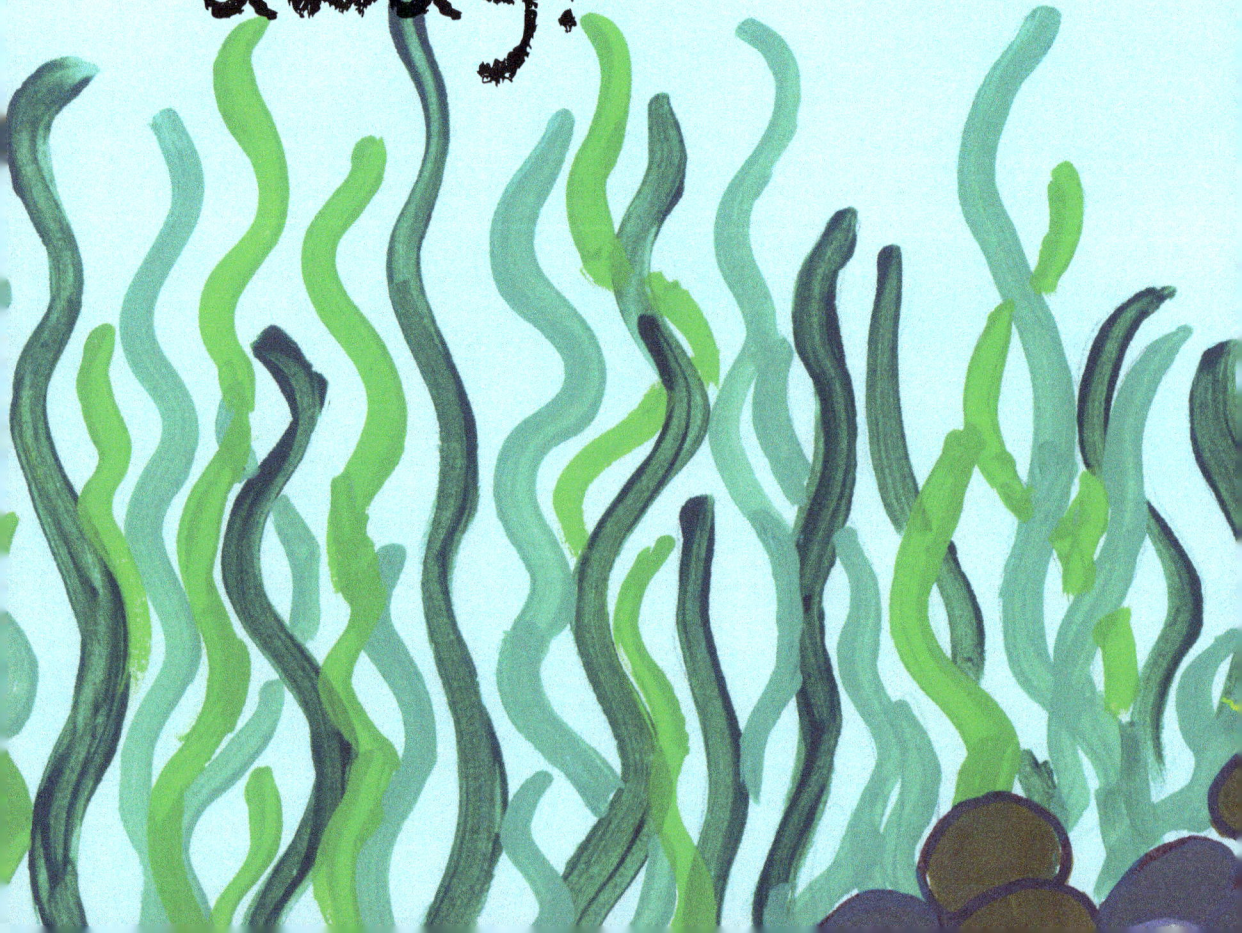

كم من الأسرار تخفيها في نفسك ؟

None!!!!!

لا شيء

Allah
AL-Aleem

الله العليم

He knows

هو يعلم

SURAH AL-AHZAAB 33:54

What will happen tomorrow or the days that follow?

ماذا يحدث غدا و بعد غد؟

1

8

9

6

10

3

No need to worry

لا تقلق

Allah Al-Aleem

الله العليم

He knows

هو يعلم

SURAH TAHA 20:110

A secret you hide in
your chest

سر تخفيه في صدرك

Or when no one sees
you behaved your
very best

لا أحد يشاهدك و انت في أحسن
حالاتك

One thing is
for sure

بالتأكيد

Allah
AL-Aleem

الله العليم

He knows

هو يعلم

SURAH AL-MA'IDAH 5:7 SURAH IBRAHIM 14:31

And He is the knower of all things.

وهو بكل شيء عليم

اَلْحَمْدُ لِلَّهِ رَبِّ الْعَالَمِينَ

www.ingramcontent.com/pod-product-compliance
Lightning Source LLC
Chambersburg PA
CBHW041634040426
42447CB00020B/3487